Asian Iconography Series-II

Three Hundred and Sixty Buddhist Deities

Compiled by
Musashi Tachikawa
Masahide Mori
Shinobu Yamaguchi

ADROIT PUBLISHERS
DELHI-110 053

Asian Iconography Series-II

Three Hundred and Sixty Buddhist Deities

Published by
ADROIT PUBLISHERS
C-8/2, Yamuna Vihar, Delhi-110 053
e-mail: akhilbooks@yahoo.com
Phone: 3266030

ISBN : 81-87392-20-7

Printed in India at
Nice Printing Press, Delhi-110 092

Foreword

This book is the second volume of *Asian Iconography Series,* which started in order to furnish materilas for iconographic studies of Hinduism and Buddhism in the spring of 2000. The first volume of the series, which is entitled "Five Hundred Buddhist Deities," has presented a collection of the black and white wooden prints of about five hundred deites of Tibetan Buddhism.

This second volume also contains an important collection of line drawings of Tibetan Buddhist deities. Since the collection contains the line drawings of about three hundred sixty Buddhist deities, it has been called "Three Hundred Sixty Buddhist Deities." The original title of the collection is given in Chinese: *Chu Fo P'u-sa Sheng Hsiang Tsan* 諸尊諸菩薩聖像贊*(The Eulogy of Sacred Images of Buddhas and Bodhisattvas).* Obviously, the collelction of Tibetan Buddhist deities was compiled in China.

The Tibeto-Chinese collection of the line drawings reproduced in the second volume of our series has been published by E. Clark in his *Two Lamaistic Pantheons* (Harvard University, 1937, pp. 225-314), although each of the drawings has been printed in a rather small size (5 x 8 cm). In the present volume the size of each drawing is enlarged (10.5 x 16 cm) so that one could see the details of each line drawing. The collection originally consists of two parts: The line drawing of each deity and the eulogy written in Chinese dedicated to each deity. Clark's book contains only the former part of the collection. In our volume, however, the eulogy part has also been included.

In the summer of 1997, I could have a chance to meet him in New Delhi. Immediately after we had discussed about iconographical studies of Buddhist Tantrism, he presented to me a complete set of the films of the *Chu Fo P'u-sa Sheng Hsiang Tsan* 諸尊諸菩薩聖像贊, i.e., the *Three Hundred Sixty Buddhist Deities.* In this volume I could thus have the previlege of useing the film which he presented to me. Here I would like to express my deepest gratitude to Dr. Lokesh Chandra, who gave me the film together with the permission of publishing it. I am also much obliged to Prof. Yasuhiko Nagano, a collegue of mine at the National Museum of Ethnology, Osaka, Japan, who enabled me to meet Dr. Lokesh Chandra at New Delhi in 1997. In Japan Prof. Nagano encouraged me to publish the *Three Hundred Sixty Buddhist Deities*.

This is a part of the research project of the National Museum of Ethnology entitled "Ethnological Studies of Healing and Salvation" (headed by M. Tachikawa, 1999-2000).
This volume ha sbeen prepared by three of us: Dr. Masahide Mori (Associate Professor, Koyasan University, Wakayama), Dr. Shinobu Yamaguchi (Associate Professor, Chukyo Women's University, Aichi), and Dr. M. Tachikawa. However, the part of the index has been prepared by Dr. Mori.

Musashi Tachikawa
Professor
National Museum of Ethnology
Osaka, Japan

Contents

Introduction

Modern scholars have called *Chu Fo P'u-sa Shêng Hsiang Tsan* as *Collection of Three Hundred Sixty Deities* (Baiei Henmi, *Chugoku Ramakyo Bijutsu Taikan* [Survey of Tibetan Buddhist Arts in China], Tokyo Bijutsu, 1975, p. 573) or 360 *Icons* (Lokesh Chandra, *Buddhist Iconography*, Aditya Prakashan, New Delhi, Vol.1, 1987, p. 6). Staël-hostein believes that the 360 *Icons* is to be ascribed to the same Lalitavajra who composed the 300 *Icons* (E. Clark, *Two Lamaistic Pantheons*, 1937, Harvard University, p. x; Sushama Lohia, *Lalitavajra's Manual of Buddhist Iconography,* International Academy of Indian Culture and Adity a Prakasham, New Delhi, 1994). However, the pantheon of the 360 *Icons* is similar to that of the 300 *Icons*, but the former is not made merely adding sixty deities to the latter.

The members of the 360 deities are classified into twenty-three groups:

I. Great Masters of Prajñāpāramitā-yāna 般若祖師
II. Great Masters of Mantra-yāna in India 秘密祖師
III. Great Masters of Mantra-yāna in Tibet 秘密道祖師
IV. Great Deities of Mantra-yāna 大秘密仏
V. Mantra-yāna Deities 諸様秘密仏
VI. Pañca-Tathāgata 五方仏
VII. Thirty-five Buddhas 三十五仏
VIII. Buddhas of Ten Directions 十方仏
IX. Six Buddhas of the Past 六勇仏（過去仏）
X. Bhaiṣajyaguru 薬師仏
XI. Buddhas 諸様仏
XII. Mañjuśrī 文殊化像菩薩
XIII. Avalokiteśvara 観世音菩薩化像
XIV. Sixteen Bodhisattvas in Vajradhātumaṇḍala 毘盧仏壇場内菩薩
XV. Bodhisattva 諸様菩薩
XVI. Pañcarakṣā 保護仏母
XVII. Tārā 救度仏母
XVIII. Female Deities 諸様仏母
XIX. Eighteen Arhats 十八羅漢
XX. Arhats 諸様羅漢
XXI. Dharmapāla 勇保護法
XXII. Vaiśravaṇa 財宝天王
XXIII. Dharmapāla 諸様護法

We had no chance to examine the original manuscript of the 360 *Icons*, i.e., *Chu Fo P'u-sa Shêng Hsiang Tsan.* Accordingly, the size or the quality of the manuscript is unknown to us. The below is the first photograph of the 360 *Icons* which Lokesh Chandra gave us.

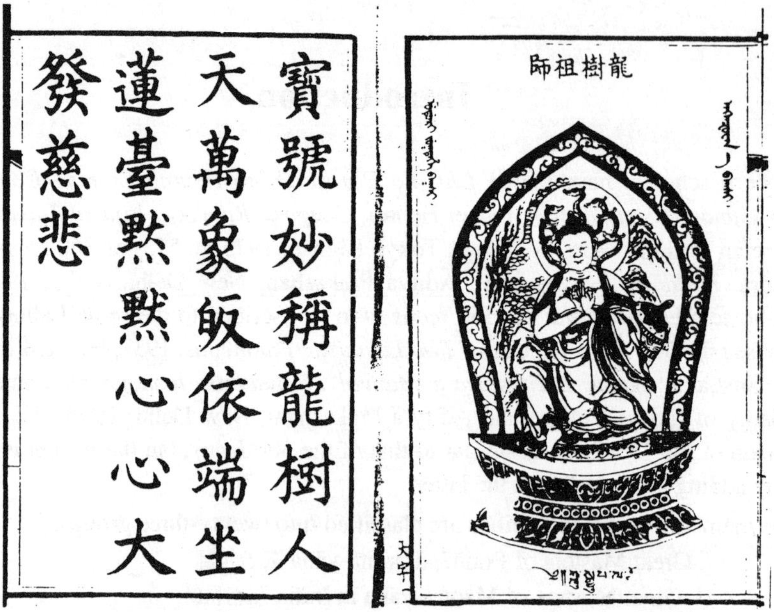

As in the same manner as the first photograph, each of the other photographs shows an icon or figure and its eulogy. Judging from the size of Chinese or Tibetan letters found in each page of the manuscript, the size of the paper is rather small.

In order to include the 360 *Icons* or *Three Hundred Sixty Buddhist Deities* in *Asian Iconography Series*, we put the figure of a deity on the above of each page, and the eulogy of the deity at the bottom of the same page.

As for the Sanskrit name of each deity, we have basically followed Clark's *Two Lamaistic Pantheon*. Further examination of Clark's identifications, and a comparative study of the pantheon of the 300 *Icons* with that of the 360 *Icons* should be carried out in the near future.

List of the Masters and Deities

I. Great Masters of Prajñāpāramitā-yāna 般若祖師

No.	Tibetan	Sanskrit
1	Klu sgrub	Nāgārjuna
2	Thogs med	Asaṅga
3	'Phags pa lha	Āryadeva
4	dByig gnyen	Vasubandhu
5	Phyogs glang	Dignāga
6	Chos grags	Dharmakīrti
7	Yon tan 'od	Guṇaprabha
8	Shā kya 'od	Śākyaprabha
9	Zla ba grags pa	Candrakīrti
10	Zhi ba lha	Śāntideva

II. Great Masters of Mantra-yāna in India 秘密祖師

No.	Tibetan	Sanskrit
11	Sa ra ha	Saraha
12	Lu hi pa	Lūhipāda
13	Dril bu pa	Ghaṇṭāpāda
14	Nag po spyod pa	Kṛṣṇacārin
15	La li ta	Lalita[vajra]
16	Ḍo mbi pa	Ḍombīpāda
17	Te lo pa	Tailakapāda
18	Nā ro pa	Nāḍapāda

III. Great Masters of Mantra-yāna in Tibet 秘密道祖師

No.	Tibetan	Sanskrit
19	Jo a ti sha	Atīśa
20	'Brom ston pa	
21	bTsong kha pa chen po	
22	rGyal tshab rje	
23	mKhas grub rje	
24	dGe 'dun grub pa	
25	rJes pan chen blo bzang chos kyi[1] rgyal mtshan	
26	rJe ngag dbang blo bzang rgyal po	
27	Pan chen blo bzang ye shes	
28	Tā la'i bla ma skal bzang rgya[2] mtsho	

IV. Great Deities of Mantra-yāna 大秘密仏

No.	Tibetan	Sanskrit
29	rGyal ba rdo rje 'chang	Vajradhara
30	gSang 'dus 'jam pa'i rdo rje	Guhyasamāja-Mañjuvajra
31	'Jam dbyangs nang sgrub	Antarasādhana-Mañjughoṣa
32	gSang 'dus mi bskyod[3] rdo rje	Guhyasamāja-Akṣobhya-vajra

[1] The caption below the figure reads kyis.
[2] Caption: rgyal.
[3] Caption: skyod.

33	gSang 'dus 'jigs rten dbang phyug	Guhyasamāja-Lokeśvara
34	sPyan ras gzigs rgyal ba rgya mtsho	Jinasāgara-Avalokiteśvara
35	Dus kyi 'khor lo	Kālacakra
36	dPal 'khor lo sdom pa	Śrīcakrasaṃvara
37	bDe mchog[4] dkar po	Sita-Saṃvara
38	bDe mchog[5] rdor sems	Vajrasattva-Saṃvara
39	bDe mchog[6] lhan skyes	Sahaja-Saṃvara
40	bDe mchog[7] mkha' lding	Garuḍa-Saṃvara?
41	rDo rje[8] khyung khra	Vajragaruḍa (śabala)?
42	'Jigs byed	Bhairava
43	dGra nag	Kṛṣṇāri?
44	gDong po drug pa	Ṣaṇmukha?
45	gShin rje[9] gshed mar	Rakta-Yamāri
46	'Jigs byed dpa' gcig	Ekavīra-Bhairava
47	Kyai rdo rje	Hevajra
48	sNying po kyai rdo rje	Garbha-Hevajra?
49	rDo rje bdud rtsi[10]	Vajrāmṛta
50	Ma hā ma ya	Mahāmāyā
51	Sangs rgyas thod pa	Buddhakapāla
52	Ye shes mkha' 'gro	Jñānaḍākinī
53	bDag med	Nairātmyā
54	rDo rje phag mo	Vajravārāhī
55	mKha' 'gro[11] ma	Ḍākinī
56	rDo rje hūṃ mdzad	Vajrahūṃkāra
57	rDo rje gdan bzhi	Vajracatuḥpīṭha
58	rNal 'byor nam mkha'	Yogāmbara
59	Phyag rdor[12] 'khor chen	Mahācakra-Vajrapāṇi?
60	Ku ru ku le	Kurukullā
61	rTa mgrin gsang sgrub	Guhyasādhana-Hayagrīva
62	rTa mgrin padma gar dbang	Padmanarteśvara-Hayagrīva

V. Mantra-yāna Deities 諸様秘密仏

63	Tshe dpag med phyag bzhi ba	Caturbhuja-Amitāyus
64	Tshe dpag med	Amitāyus
65	rDo rje dbyings	Vajradhātu
66	rNam[13] snang shā kya seng ge	Vairocana-Śākyasiṃha
67	Chos dbyings[14] gsung gi dbang phyug	Dharmadhātuvāgīśvara

[4] Caption: mchogs.
[5] Caption: mchogs.
[6] Caption: mchogs.
[7] Caption: mchogs.
[8] Caption: rjes.
[9] Caption: rjes.
[10] Caption: rtsis.
[11] The caption adds spyod below 'gro ma.
[12] Caption: tor.
[13] Caption: rnams.
[14] Caption: dbying.

68	Kun rig rnam[15] par snang mdzad	Sarvavid-Vairocana
69	rDo rje sems dpa'	Vajrasattva
70	rNam snang mngon byang[16]	Vairocanābhisambodhi
71	Phyag rdor 'byung po 'dul byed	Bhūtaḍāmara-Vajrapāṇi
72	Phyag rdor gos sngon can	Nīlāmbaradhara-Vajrapāṇi?
73	Phyag rdor gtum chung	Caṇḍa-Vajrapāṇi
74	Phyag rdor u tsa rya	Ucchraya(?)-Vajrapāṇi
75	gTum po zhal gsum phyag drug pa	Trimukhaṣaḍbhuja-Caṇḍa
76	rTa mgrin lcags ral can	Hayagrīva?

VI. Pañca-Tathāgata 五方仏

77	rNam snang	Vairocana
78	Mi bskyod pa	Akṣobhya
79	Rin 'byung	Ratnasambhava
80	'Od dpag med	Amitābha
81	Don 'grub	Amoghasiddhi

VII. Thirty-five Buddhas 三十五仏

82	Shā kya thub pa	Śākyamuni
83	rDo rje'i snying pos rab tu 'joms pa	Vajragarbhapramardin
84	Rin chen 'od 'phro[17]	Ratnārcis
85	Klu dbang gi rgyal po	Nāgeśvararāja
86	dPa' bo'i sde	Vīrasena
87	dPal dgyes	Vīranandin
88	Rin chen me	Ratnāgni
89	Rin chen zla 'od	Ratnacandraprabha
90	mThong ba don yod	Amoghadarśin
91	Rin chen zla ba	Ratnacandra
92	Dri ma med pa	Vimala
93	dPal byin	Śūradatta
94	Tshangs pa	Brahmā
95	Tshangs pas byin	Brahmadatta
96	Chu lha	Varuṇa
97	Chu lha'i lha	Varuṇadeva
98	dPal bzang	Bhadraśrī
99	Tsan dan dpal	Candanaśrī
100	gZi brjid mtha' yas	Anantaujas
101	'Od dpal	Prabhāsaśrī
102	Mya ngan med pa'i dpal	Aśokaśrī
103	Sred med kyi bu	Nārāyaṇa
104	Me tog dpal	Kusumaśrī
105	Tshangs pa'i 'od zer rnam par rol bas mngon par mkhyen pa	Brahmajyotirvikrīḍitābhijña
106	Padma'i 'od zer rnam par rol bas mngon par	Padmajyotirvikrīḍitābhijña

[15]Caption: rnams.
[16]Caption: rNams snang mngon byangs.
[17]Caption: 'phros.

	mkhyen pa	
107	Nor dpal	Dhanaśrī
108	Dran pa'i dpal	Smṛtiśrī
109	mTshan dpal shin tu yongs sbgrags	Suparikīrtitanāmaśrī
110	dBang po'i tog gi rgyal mtshan gyi rgyal po	Indraketudhvajarāja
111	Shin tu rnam par gnon pa'i dpal	Suvikrāntaśrī
112	g'Yul las shin tu rnam par rgyal ba	Yuddhajaya
113	rNam par gnon pa'i gshegs pa'i dpal	Vikrāntagāmiśrī
114	Kun nas snang ba bkod pa'i dpal	Samantāvabhāsavyūhaśrī
115	Rin chen padmas rnam par gnon pa	Ratnapadmavikrāmin
116	Sangs rgyas ri dbang gi rgyal po	Śailendrarāja

VIII. Buddhas of Ten Directions 十方仏

117	Sangs rgyas rje su spyod pa	Anucārin?-Buddha
118	Sangs rgyas mngon 'phags rgyal po	Abhyudgatarāja-Buddha
119	'Khon dang (?) rgyags pa rnam gnon	
120	Sangs rgyas rin chen gzugs bkod 'od snang	Ratnāṅgavyūhadyuti-Buddha
121	Sangs rgyas bdud dang yid gnyis kun 'joms (?)	
122	Phyir mi ldog pa'i 'khor lo 'byung ba'i dpal	Avaivartikacakrasambhava-śrī?
123	Sangs rgyas rin gdugs 'phags	Ratnacchattrodgata-Buddha
124	Sangs rgyas byang sems 'dul ba	
125	sKrag med mun bral rgyal po	Nirbhayavigatatamorāja?
126	Dang po sems skyed the tshom gcod mdzad	Prathamacittotpādasaṃ-śayacchedika?

IX. Six Buddhas of the Past 六勇仏（過去仏）

127	Sangs rgyas rnam gzigs	Vipaśyin
128	gTsug tor can	Śikhin
129	Thams cad skyob	Viśvabhū
130	'Khor ba 'jig	Krakucchanda
131	gSer thub	Kanakamuni
132	'Od bsrung	Kāśyapa

X. Bhaiṣajyaguru 薬師仏

133	mTshan legs yongs grags dpal gyi rgyal po	Suparikīrtitanāmaśrīrāja
134	Sangs rgyas rin po che dang zla ba dang padmas rab tu brgyan pa mkhas pa gzi brjid sgra dbyangs kyi rgyal po	Ratnacandrapadmaprati-maṇḍitapaṇḍita?tejaḥsvara-ghoṣarāja
135	gSer bzang dri med rin chen snang brtul zhugs pa	Suvarṇabhadravimalaratna-prabhāsavrata
136	Mya ngan med mchog[18] dpal	Aśokottamaśrī
137	Chos sgrags rgya mtsho'i dbyang	Dharmakīrtisāgaraghoṣa
138	Chos rgya mtsho mchog gi blos rnam par rol bar mngon par mkhyen pa'i rgyal po	Dharmasāgarāgra?mati-vikrīḍitābhijñārāja

[18]Caption: mchogs.

139	sMan gyi bla bai dū rya'i 'od kyi rgyal po	Bhaiṣajyaguru-Vaiḍūrya-prabhārāja

XI. Buddhas 諸様仏

140	rGyal ba seng ge'i nga ro	Siṃhanāda
141	rDo rje mi 'khrugs pa	Vajrākṣobhya
142	'Od zer kun 'phags dpal brtsegs[19] rgyal po	Raśmisamudgataśrīkūṭarāja
143	rGyal ba kun gzigs	Samantadarśin
144	Rin chen gtsug tor can	Ratnaśikhin

XII. Mañjuśrī 文殊化像菩薩

145	'Jam dbyangs dkar po	Sita-Mañjughoṣa
146	'Jam dbyangs[20] dpal gzhon nur gyur ba	Kumārabhūta-Mañjuśrī
147	'Jam dbyangs brtan pa'i 'khor lo	Sthiracakra-Mañjughoṣa
148	'Jam dbyangs[21] gsang sgrub	Guhyasādhana-Mañjughoṣa
149	'Jam dbyangs[22] seng ge'i sgra	Siṃhanāda-Mañjughoṣa
150	'Jam dbyangs[23] ngag gi rgyal po	Vādirāḍ-Mañjughoṣa
151	'Jam dbyangs chos dbyings gsung gi dbang phyug brgyad pa	Aṣṭabhuja-Dharmadhātu-vāgīśvara-Mañjughoṣa
152	'Jam dbyangs sgra bzang dbang phyug rgyal po	Bhadrasvareśvararāja-Mañjughoṣa
153	'Jam[24] dpal rgyal po rol ba	Rājalīlā-Mañjuśrī
154	'Jig gsum lhag par dbang du byed pa'i 'jam dbyangs	Trailokyavaśyādhikāra-Mañjughoṣa
155	mTshan brjod kyi 'jam dbyangs phyag bzhi pa	Caturbhuja-Nāmasaṃgīti-Mañjughoṣa
156	'Jam dbyangs shes rab 'khor lo dang po	Prajñācakra-Mañjughoṣa
157	'Jam dpal rnon po	Ṭīkṣṇa-Mañjuśrī

XIII. Avalokiteśvara 観世音菩薩化像

158	sPyan ras gzigs phyag bzhi pa	Caturbhuja-Avalokiteśvara
159	sPyan ras gzigs padma dbang 'byed	Padmavikāsana-Avalokiteśvara
160	sPyan ras gzigs kha sar pa ni	Khasarpaṇa-Avalokiteśvara
161	sPyan ras gzigs seng ge'i sgra	Siṃhanāda-Avalokiteśvara
162	'Jig rten dbang phyug halhala	Hālāhala-Lokeśvara
163	sPyan ras gzigs rdo rje chos	Vajradharma-Avalokiteśvara
164	sPyan ras gzigs padma gar dbang phyag gnyis pa	Dvibhuja-Padmanarteśvara-Avalokiteśvara
165	Padma gar dbang phyag bco brgyad pa	Aṣṭadaśabhuja-Padmanarteśvara

---

[19]Caption: brtsags.
[20]Caption: omits dbyangs.
[21]Caption: dbyang.
[22]Caption: dbyang.
[23]Caption: dbyang.
[24]Caption: 'Jams.

166	'Jig rten dbang phyug ha ri ha ri la zhon pa	Hariharivāhana-Lokeśvara
167	Khams gsum dbang 'dus spyan ras gzigs	Trailokyavaśaṃkara-Avalokiteśvara
168	'Jig rten dbang phyug dmar po phyag bzhi pa	Caturbhuja-rakta-Lokeśvara
169	'Jig rten dbang phyug mgrin sngon can	Nīlakaṇṭha-Lokeśvara
170	sGyu 'phrul[25] dra ba'i rim pa'i spyan ras gzigs	Māyājālakrama-Avalokiteśvara
171	Don yod zhags pa	Amoghapāśa
172	sPyan ras gzigs bhu kham dmar po	Mahābhūmika?-rakta-Avalokiteśvara
173	bCu gcig zhal	Ekādaśamukha[-Avalokiteśvara]
174	Nam mkha'[26] rgyal po	Gaganarāja
175	sPyan ras gzigs sems nyid ngal gso	Cittaviśrāmaṇa-Avalokiteśvara
176	sPyan ras gzigs yid bzhin nor bu	Cintāmaṇi-Avalokiteśvara
177	sPyan ras gzigs rdo rje[27] snying pos rab tu 'joms pa	Vajragarbhapramardin-Avalokiteśvara

XIV. Sixteen Bodhisattvas in Vajradhātumaṇḍala 毘盧仏壇場内菩薩

178	rDo rje khu tshur	Vajramuṣṭi
179	rDo rje gnod sbyin	Vajrayakṣa
180	rDo rje bsrung	Vajrarakṣa
181	rDo rje las	Vajrakarma
182	rDo rje smra ba	Vajrabhāṣa
183	rDo rje rgyu	Vajrahetu
184	rDo rje rnon po	Vajratīkṣṇa
185	rDo rje chos	Vajradharma
186	rDo rje bzhad pa	Vajrahāsa
187	rDo rje rgyal mtshan	Vajraketu
188	rDo rje gzi brjid	Vajratejas
189	rDo rje rin chen	Vajraratna
190	rDo rje legs pa	Vajrasādhu
191	rDo rje chags pa	Vajrarāga
192	rDo rje rgyal po	Vajrarāja
193	Byang chub rdo rje sems dpa'	Vajrasattva Bodhisattva

XV. Bodhisattva 諸様菩薩

194	Byams pa phyag bzhi pa	Caturbhuja-Maitreya
195	Byams pa phyag gnyis pa	Dvibhuja-Maitreya
196	Nam mkha'[28] snying po	Ākāśagarbha
197	Sa'i snying po	Kṣitigarbha
198	Kun tu bzang po	Samantabhadra

[25] Clark's index: 'phul.
[26] Caption: mkhas.
[27] Clark's index: rje'i.
[28] Caption: mkha'i.

199	sGrib pa rnam sel	Sarvanivaraṇaviṣkambhin
200	Kun tu bzang po glang chen po	Hastivāhana-Samanta-bhadra

XVI. Pañcarakṣā 保護仏母

201	sTong chen mo	Mahāsāhasrapramardanī
202	rMa bya chen mo[29]	Mahāmāyūrī
203	bSil ba'i tshal	Śītavatī
204	gSang sngags rjes 'dzin	Mantrānusāriṇī
205	So sor 'brangs ma	Pratisarā

XVII. Tārā 救度仏母

206	Seng ldeng nag 'bye sgrol ma	Khadiravaṇī-Tārā
207	Myur shing dpa'i sgrol ma	Pravīra?-Tārā
208	sGrol ma zla mdang ma	Candrakānti?-Tārā
209	sGrol ma gser mdog ma	Kanakavarṇa-Tārā
210	gTsug tor sgrol ma	Uṣṇīṣa-Tārā
211	sGrol ma hūṃ sgra sgrogs ma	Hūṃsvaranādinī-Tārā
212	rNam par rgyal ba'i sgrol ma	Vijaya-Tārā
213	sGrol ma gzhan gyis mi thub pa	Aparājita-Tārā
214	sGrol ma bdud 'joms ma	Mārasūdana-Tārā
215	Mya ngan sel ba'i sgrol ma	Śokavinodana-Tārā
216	'Gro ba 'gugs pa'i sgrol ma	Jagadvaśī?-Tārā
217	bKra shis skye ba'i sgrol ma	Maṅgalotpādana-Tārā
218	sGrol ma smin byed ma	Pācaka-Tārā
219	sGrol ma khros ma nag mo	Kruddha-kālī-Tārā
220	Zhi ba[30] chen mo'i sgrol ma	Mahāśānti-Tārā
221	Chags pa 'joms pa'i sgrol ma	Rāganisūdana-Tārā
222	bDe ba sbyin pa'i sgrol mo	Sukhada-Tārā
223	sGrol ma rnam par rgyal ma dkar mo	Sita-Vijaya-Tārā
224	sDug bsngal bsregs pa'i sgrol ma	Duḥkhadahana-Tārā
225	dNgos grub stsol ba'i sgrol ma	Siddhida-Tārā
226	Yongs su rdzogs pa'i sgrol ma	Paripūrṇa-Tārā?
227	Dug[31] nag sel ba'i sgrol ma	Jāṅgulī-Tārā

XVIII. Female Deities 諸様仏母

228	Gur las gzungs pa'i rdo rje sgrol ma	[Vajra]pañjarabhāṣita-Vajratārā
229	rGya nag rim pa'i sgrol ma	Cīnakrama-Tārā
230	sGrol dkar yid bzhin gyi 'khor lo	Cintāmaṇicakra-sita-Tārā
231	Yid bzhin rgyal mo phyag bzhi ma	Caturbhuja-Cintāmaṇirājñī
232	sGrol dkar phyag drug ma	Ṣaḍbhuja-sita-Tārā
233	sGrol ma nor sbyin ma	Dhanada-Tārā
234	Ngan song las sgrol ba'i sgrol ma	Durgottāriṇī-Tārā

[29]Caption: po.
[30]Caption: ba'i.
[31]Caption: bDug.

235	Don thams cad sgrub pa'i sgrol ma	Sarvārthasādhana-Tārā
236	'Phags ma dug sel ma	Ārya-Jāṅgulī
237	lHa mo ral gcig phyag nyi shu rtsa bzhi ma	Caturviṃśatibhuja-Ekajaṭā
238	sNa chogs yum	Viśvamātṛ
239	lHa mo ral gcig ma	Ekajaṭā
240	lHa mo tsundā phyag bzhi ma	Caturbhuja-Cundā
241	lHa mo tsundā phyag mang	Bahubhuja-Cundā
242	'Od zer can phyag bcu ma	Daśabhuja-Mārīcī
243	'Od zer can phyag brgyad ma	Aṣṭabhuja-Mārīcī
244	'Od zer can phyag gnyis ma	Dvibhuja-Mārīcī
245	'Od zer can bdud rtsi'i ma	Mārīcī
246	'Od zer can rdo rje dbyings kyi dbang phyug ma	Vajradhātvīśvarī-Mārīcī
247	gTsug tor rnam[32] rgyal ma	Uṣṇīṣavijayā
248	'Phags ma gdugs dkar po can	Ārya-Sitātapatrā
249	Lo ma gyon ma phyag drug ma	Ṣaḍbhuja-Parṇaśabarī
250	Lo ma gyon ma phyag bzhi ma	Caturbhuja-Parṇaśabarī[33]
251	Sher phyin phyag gnyis ma	Dvibhuja-Prajñāpāramitā
252	Sher phyin phyag bzhi ma	Caturbhuja-Prajñāpāramitā
253	rDo rje dbyangs can ma phyag drug ma	Ṣaḍbhuja-Vajrasarasvatī
254	rDo rje dbyangs can ma phyag gnyis ma	Dvibhuja-Vajrasarasvatī
255	Pi wang dbyangs can ma	Vīṇā-Sarasvatī
256	lHa mo khro gnyer can	Bhṛkuṭī
257	rDo rje tsa rtsig[34]	Vajracarcikā
258	Sor 'brangs phyag gnyis ma	Dvibhuja-Pratisarā
259	Phyir bzlog ma	Mahāpratyaṅgirā
260	rGyal mtshan rtse mo'i dpung rgyan	Dhvajāgrakeyūrā
261	gZhan gyis mi thub ma	Aparājitā
262	rDo rje gandha ri	Vajragāndhārī
263	Chos kyi rdo rje ma	Dharmavajrī
264	Las kyi rdo rje ma	Karmavajrī
265	Sems ma rdo rje ma	Sattvavajrī
266	Rin chen rdo rje ma	Ratnavajrī
267	lHa mo shra ma ṇa	Śramaṇā
268	Nor sbyin ma	Dhanadā
269	gZa' yum	Grahamātṛkā
270	Pad dkar shes rab gsal byed	Prajñālokakṛtya-sita-Vajravārāhī
271	Phag mo don thams cad sgrub pa	Sarvārthasādhana-Vārāhī

XIX. Eighteen Arhats 十八羅漢

272	Yan lag 'byung	Aṅgaja
273	Ma pham pa	Ajita
274	Nags na gnas	Vaṇavāsin
275	Dus ldan	Kālika

[32]Caption: rnams.

[33]Ch. 二臂. The deity is depicted in two-armed figure.

[34]Clark's index: rtsiga.

276 rDo rje mo'i bu — Vajrīputra
277 bZang po — Bhadra
278 gSer bi'u — Kanakavatsa
279 Ba ra dhwā dza gser can — Kanakabharadvāja
280 Ba ku la — Bakula
281 sGra gcan 'dzin — Rāhula
282 Lam phran — Cūḍapanthaka
283 Ba ra dhwā dza bsdod snyoms les — Piṇḍolabharadvāja
284 Lam bstan — Panthaka
285 Klu'i sde — Nāgasena
286 sBed byed pa — Gopaka
287 Mi phyed pa — Abheda
288 dGe bsnyen dharma ta la — Upāsaka-Dharmatāla
289 Hwa shang dge bsnyen — Upāsaka-Hwa-shang

XX. Arhats 諸樣羅漢

290 'Od bsrung chen po — Mahākāśyapa
291 Kun dga' bo — Ānanda
292 Sha na'i gos can — Śāṇakavāsin
293 Nyer sbas — Upagupta
294 Dhi dhi ka — Dhītika
295 Nag po — Kāla
296 Legs mthong — Sudarśana

XXI. Dharmapāla 勇保護法

297 mGon po phyag drug pa — Ṣaḍbhuja-Mahākāla
298 'Brong zhal can
299 Ṭa kṣad seng ge zhon pa — Siṃhavāhana-Ṭakṣad
300 mGon po ṭa kṣad-? — Mahākāla-Ṭakṣad
301 mGon po stag zhon — Vyāghravāhana-Mahākāla
302 mGon po legs ldan — Bhagavad-Mahākāla
303 mGon po beng — Daṇḍa[dhara]-Mahākāla
304 Las mgon bya rog gdong can — Kākāsya-Karmanātha
305 mGon po gur — Mahākāla-pañjara?
306 mGon po phyag bzhi pa — Caturbhuja-Mahākāla
307 Zhal bram gzugs — Brāhmaṇarūpa[-Mahākāla]
308 Ṭa kṣad nag po — Kṛṣṇa-Ṭakṣad
309 lHa mo dong skyong ma — Śaṅkhapālī
310 lHa mo dong sol ma — Dhūmāvatī
311 dPal ldan lha mo phyag gnyis ma — Dvibhuja-śrīmatī-Devī
312 Chos rgyal — Dharmarāja
313 Ṭa kki ra dza — Ṭakkirāja
314 Dzi na mi ṭra — Jinamitra
315 Kṣe tra pa la — Kṣetrapāla
316 Tshe bdag mgon po[35] — Āyuṣpati-Mahākāla

[35]Caption: pa.

317	mGon dkar yid bzhin nor bu	Sita-Cintāmaṇi-Mahākāla

XXII. Vaiśravaṇa 財宝天王

318	rNam sras tshe 'phel dkar po	Sita-Āyurvardhana-Vaiśravaṇa
319	rNam sras drag byed nag po	Raudra-kṛṣṇa-Vaiśravaṇa
320	rGyal chen rnam thos sras	Mahārāja-Vaiśravaṇa
321	rNam sras mdong dmar	Raktaśūla-Vaiśravaṇa
322	rNam sras ser chen	Mahāpīta-Vaiśravaṇa

XXIII. Dharmapāla 諸様護法

323	Sa'i lha mo brtan ma	Dṛḍhā-Pṛthivī
324	rNam sras gar mkhan mchog	Nartakavara-Vaiśravaṇa
325	'Phags skyes po	Virūḍhaka
326	sPyan mi bzang	Virūpākṣa
327	Yul 'khor bsrung	Dhṛtarāṣṭra
328	brGya byin	Śatakratu
329	Tshangs pa	Brahman
330	lHa mo tsaṇḍi ka	Caṇḍikā
331	dPyid kyi lha mo	Vasanta-devī
332	dByar gyi lha mo	Varṣā-devī
333	sTon gyi lha mo	Śarad-devī
334	dGun gyi lha mo	Hemanta-devī
335	bKra shis tshe ring ma	Maṅgaladīrghāyus
336	Beg tse	
337	Dur khrod bdag po	Citipati
338	Mi g'yo ba sngon po	Nīla-Acala
339	Dzam bha la ser po	Pīta-Jambhala
340	Mi g'yo ba dkar po	Sita-Acala
341	Dzam bha la phyag drug pa	Ṣaḍbhuja-Jambhala
342	Khro bo stobs po che	Krodhamahābala
343	'Jig rten gsum rgyal	Trailokyavijaya
344	Dzam bha la nag po	Kṛṣṇa-Jambhala
345	Gegs mthar byed	Vighnāntaka
346	bDud rtsi 'khyil pa	Amṛtakuṇḍalin
347	rDo rje lcags sgrog ma[36]	Vajraśṛṅkhalā
348	Mi g'yo ba spre'u brgyad pa	Aṣṭakapi-Acala
349	Me ltar 'bar ba	Jvālānala
350	Mi g'yo ba phyag bzhi pa	Caturbhuja-Acala
351	Khro mo sme brtsegs	
352	rDo rje rnam 'joms	Vajravidāraṇī
353	Zhang blon rdo rje bdud 'dul	
354	gNod sbyin gang ba bzang po	Yakṣa-Pūrṇabhadra
355	Dzam bha la dkar po 'brug zhon	Sita-nāgavāhana-Jambhala
356	Khro bo sme[37] brtsegs	

[36]Caption: omits ma.
[37]Caption: me.

357	Seng gdong ma	Siṃhavaktrā
358	bCom ldan reg tshig	Bhagavad-Bhayanāśana
359	rDo rje hūṃ mdzad	Vajrahūṃkāra
360	Tshogs bdag dmar chen	Mahārakta-Gaṇapati

References

Clark, Walter Eugene, *Two Lamaistic Pantheons*. 2 vols. Harvard-Yenching Institute Monograph Series, Vol. III. Cambridge, Massachusetts: Harvard University Press, 1937.

Figures and Eulogies

1 Klu sgrub
Nāgārjuna

寶號妙稱龍樹人
天萬象皈依端坐
蓮臺默默心心大
發慈悲

2 Thogs med
Asaṅga

自是西方大覺慧
根六塵俱脱看破
五蘊皆空祖師一
毫無着

3 ’Phags pa lha
Āryadeva

瞻仰金容藹吉佛
門功德無邊成就
梵王妙果當號祖
師聖天

4 dByig gnyen
Vasubandhu

默捧金經一卷慈
恩不可思議瞻禮
田親祖師願授如
来妙諦

5 Phyogs glang
Dignāga

頂禮祖師明象法
界慧燈朗朗現此
妙光無兩萬代衆
生景仰

静裡海潮音泛祖
師寶號法聲仗此
無聲梵唄慈悲好
度衆生

6 Chos grags
Dharmakīrti

7 Yon tan 'od
Guṇaprabha

跏趺證果西方念
念不捨法王佛恩
萬刼難忘祖師闡
發德光

8 Shā kya 'od
Śākyaprabha

湛然獨坐寶床慧
眼遍觀十方傳布
釋迦之光祖師妙
道無疆

端然湛湛如如慧
眼大開青目祖師
無盡宏慈億兆受
茲遐福

9 Zla ba grags pa
Candrakīrti

默持佛印端然千秋寶相留傳共尊祖師善天宏仁普被大千

10 Zhi ba lha
Śāntideva

11 Sa ra ha
Saraha

凛鬚眉懾惡魔拈
一矢妙用多寶礶
裡貯金波度衆生
樂安和

祖師金身無垢持
得蛇兒在手却是
把来入口試他有
毒没有

12 Lu hi pa
Lūhipāda

13 Dril bu pa
Ghaṇṭāpāda

問寶號甘扎巴祖
師位寶堪誇持鈴
杵退魔邪使觀者
敬畏加

14 Nag po spyod pa
Kṛṣṇacārin

祖師鉢中何有可
是非空即色若能
空色两忘方知鉢
中消息

15 La li ta
Lalita[vajra]

露體一絲不掛本来面目可覩若非行滿功圓馬得成佛作祖

16 Ḍo mbi pa
Ḍombīpāda

座下調伏山君祖
師莊嚴妙相手中
法寶長持濟度永
無盡藏

莊嚴也自尋常自
具慧心大德昂然
鬚髮垂垂端居不
動聲色

17 Te lo pa
Tailakapāda

赤着身無一絲深意存知者寡那羅巴祖師號佛門中大器也

18 Nā ro pa
Nāḍapāda

手內作何佛印塔
中舍利有否要問
祖師端的不過點
頭搖首

19 Jo a ti sha
Atīśa

祖師法像年少端
坐拈花微笑看慈
歡喜形容了悟佛
門靈竅

20 'Brom ston pa

21 bTsong kha pa chen po

琪卉靈葩圍繞端
然穩坐蓮花千秋
善男信女盡頂禮
宗喀巴

22 rGyal tshab rje

膝上卷内何經不知有字無字若是無字金經還求祖師見賜

23 mKhas grub rje

座放蓮花端坐看
来好箇觀贍祖師
金身半袒不離西
域莊嚴

24 dGe 'dun grub pa

出世本具慈悲大
教演從西藏傳来
代代不磨功徳無
休難量

25 rJes pan chen blo bzang chos kyi rgyal mshan

佛土傳来手印曇
花旁列芬芳尊者
具何根行佳名萬
古傳揚

26 rJe ngag dbang blo bzang rgyal po

無字經手中持妙
蓮花掌上現轉五
輩住人間度衆生
宏誓願

27 Pan chen blo bzang ye shes

一手托定金鉢一
手拈来佛印功果
妙證梵天誰不皈
依敬信

實號雖云有異本是我佛住世常向閻浮界中要使衆生樂利

28 Tā la'i bla ma skal bzang rgya mtsho

29 rGyal ba rdo rje 'chang
Vajradhara

毫光四射無際乂
手鈴杵雙持證得
金剛大號千秋共
仰慈悲

金剛文殊秘密成
佛作祖法力妙像
阿誰柰得果證無
聲無色

30 gSang 'dus 'jam pa'i rdo rje
Guhyasamāja-Mañjuvajra

31 ’Jam dbyangs nang sgrub
Antarasādhana-Mañjughoṣa

功德威嚴浩渺文
殊寶號精明可是
神通無限諸般毒
惡潛形

不動難分爾我金
剛秘密誰知悟得
此中妙理方知我
佛慈悲

32 gSang ’dus mi bskyod rdo rje
Guhyasamāja-Akṣobhyavajra

静裡觀觀自在真
秘密誰叅解智珠
明神通大端坐在
極樂界

33 gSang 'dus 'jigs rten dbang phyug
Guhyasamāja-Lokeśvara

34 sPyan ras gzigs rgyal ba rgya mtsho
Jinasāgara-Avalokiteśvara

世音不以耳聽佛
海觀音獨步金身
意外莊嚴消息阿
誰能悟

35 Dus kyi 'khor lo
Kālacakra

幻化身外之身能使大地生春時時慧輪常轉救拔一切沉淪

極樂從来無上上
樂是何形狀悟得
上樂真形何非上
樂本相

36 dPal 'khor lo sdom pa
Śrīcakrasaṃvara

他是我我是他魔
即佛佛即魔上樂
王共合和真趣味
伊知麼

37 bDe mchog dkar po
Sita-Saṃvara

面面照臨十地手
手堅持法器勇識
上樂王佛鴻慈無
所不備

38 bDe mchog rdor sems
Vajrasattva-Saṃvara

39 bDe mchog lhan skyes
Sahaja-Saṃvara

本生上樂王佛萬古聲名赫奕任他魔怪糾纏遇了神威歛迹

猙獰法體堅剛慧
力鬼伏神降在我
佛極樂鄉稱大鵬
上樂王

40 bDe mchog mkha' lding
Garuḍa-Saṃvara?

雙展摩空羽翼不
亞孔雀明王大鵬
金剛威力証成佛
果西方

41 rDo rje khyung khra
Vajragaruḍa (śabala)?

42 'Jigs byed
Bhairava

多足多臂多首幻
像莊嚴知否妙哉
果是金剛萬古名
傳不朽

瞻黑敵威羅瓦般
般佛寶手把金剛
不壞身軀好使衆
生心寫

43 dGra nag
Kṛṣṇāri?

44 gDong po drug pa
Ṣaṇmukha?

六面六臂六足威
羅瓦金剛體般般
佛寶加持好把群
魔净洗

45 gShin rje gshed mar
Rakta-Yamāri

紅威羅瓦金剛莊嚴度世皮囊卧牛足踏當場妙哉歡喜吉祥

46 'Jigs byed dpa' gcig
Ekavīra-Bhairava

金剛身天龍首一
勇威垂悠久如来
寶常在手除魔怪
功不朽

47 Kyai rdo rje
Hevajra

消除煩惱稱喜座
上無分彼此透得
金剛意指方算佛
門弟子

48 sNying po kyai rdo rje
Garbha-Hevajra?

多目遍觀四大衆
手羣擎法寶喜心
喜得心喜萬刧永
無煩惱

49 rDo rje bdud rtsi
Vajrāmṛta

巍巍一箇金身化
現天魔歸附宏慈
度脱群迷大地遍
沾甘露

50 Ma hā ma ya
Mahāmāyā

金剛尊名大幻立
定金身璀璨要知
法度有緣可是超
登彼岸

51 Sangs rgyas thod pa
Buddhakapāla

省得金剛形狀許
汝佛門一望若是
錯認金剛可是自
生孽障

馴得靈獅座下一吼動地驚天智慧空行佛母度人無量無邊

52 Ye shes mkha' 'gro
Jñānaḍākinī

53 bDag med Nairātmyā

佛母萬千變化法
相莊嚴妙可原来
一視同仁慈念原
無爾我

54 rDo rje phag mo
Vajravārāhī

敬睹金剛亥母甘露一盂在手佛門萬劫常存任他烏飛兎走

55 mKha’ ’gro ma
Ḍākinī

赤體一絲不沾行
脚無分昏旦執着
佛母空行可是佛
門癡漢

56 rDo rje hūṃ mdzad
Vajrahūṃkāra

金剛吽聲威猛此
音那個能省座中
旁列一尊同至如
来聖境

57 rDo rje gdan bzhi
Vajracatuḥpīṭha

金剛號為四座毫
無矯揉造作能把
趣味叅破不離行
住坐卧

58 rNal 'byor nam mkha'
Yogāmbara

幻化金身顯像我
佛何等慈悲若悟
箇中滋味還須靜
裏追思

59 Phyag rdor 'khor chen
Mahācakra-Vajrapāṇi?

毒蛇伏惡魔降威
神力頌金剛大輪
轉護法王度衆生
德無疆

60 Ku ru ku le
Kurukullā

看去雕弓滿月一
矢懾服諸怪佛母
智行妙高端居蓮
花世界

61 rTa mgrin gsang sgrub
Guhyasādhana-Hayagrīva

金剛馬頭作冠由
来意馬牢跧六蘊
皆空誰悟黒漆桶
内盤桓

62 rTa mgrin padma gar dbang
Padmanarteśvara-Hayagrīva

布袋無窮妙用包
藏百二山河鎮日
大開笑口看他日
月如梭

四臂撐持九有慈
悲超度萬物陰陽
顯化一身尊稱無
量壽佛

63 Tshe dpag med phyag bzhi ba
Caturbhuja-Amitāyus

64 Tshe dpag med
Amitāyus

功德普被十方慈
輝垂布汪洋無量
壽佛恩光衆生萬
代稱揚

65 rDo rje dbyings
Vajradhātu

圓首露得多面不
論向背都見六臂
法寶持来金剛性
中操鍊

祇園普放光華頂
禮宏光釋迦慈悲
無量無涯功德遍
滿恒沙

66 rNam snang shā kya seng ge
Vairocana-Śākyasiṃha

67 Chos dbying gsung gi dbang phyug
Dharmadhātuvāgīśvara

法性無異智性妙
音即是潮音自在
西方吾佛善哉一
片婆心

68 Kun rig rnam par snang mdzad
Sarvavid-Vairocana

手執法輪常轉普
慧宏光不淺邪魔
外道俱遣遍體毫
光大展

69 rDo rje sems dpa'
Vajrasattva

妙哉金剛勇識西
土稱佛作祖憐渠
不鮮禪宗瞎證盲
叅最苦

70 rNam snang mngon byang
Vairocanābhisambodhi

善根結就菩提堪
稱宏光顯耀至誠
頂禮慈輝覺路金
繩普照

71 Phyag rdor ’byung po ’dul byed
Bhūtaḍāmara-Vajrapāṇi

両手護持佛印修
成慧力功多果證
靈山勝境維持正
道伏魔

72 Phyag rdor gos sngon can
Nīlāmbaradhara-Vajrapāṇi?

青衣手持金剛永
作西方護法慈容
煞是威嚴好把羣
迷救拔

73 Phyag rdor gtum chung
Caṇḍa-Vajrapāṇi

威烈手持金剛莊
嚴何等堂皇金鈴
寶杵叮噹護法佛
門永慶

74 Phyag rdor u tsa rya
Ucchraya(?)-Vajrapāṇi

法相猙獰端儼智
行萬年自顯能使
惡邪迹歛金剛功
德不淺

75 gTum po zhal gsum phyag drug pa
Trimukhaṣaḍbhuja-Caṇḍa

瞻仰金剛威烈三
頭六臂昂然掃盡
騰蛇毒焰優游化
日光天

76 rTa mgrin lcags ral can
Hayagrīva?

鐵劍馬頭金剛降
伏魔怪威彰神功
非比尋常萬年姓
字馨香

77 rNam snang
Vairocana

妙相端莊方正萬
古稱佛稱聖只仲
二指示人務要追
求畢竟

78 Mi bskyod pa
Akṣobhya

不動方能有動我
佛慈悲面孔衆生
領畧佛心方能開
得懺懂

79 Rin 'byung
Ratnasambhava

人見佛手無寶詑
異何稱寶勝要知
此寶根由面壁三
年再定

80 ’Od dpag med
Amitābha

阿彌陀佛稱呼若大若小都曉曉得此號者多叅透此號者少

此尊佛稱成就與
天地同萬壽叅中
宵禮白晝敬皈依
祈保佑

81 Don 'grub
Amoghasiddhi

82 Shā kya thub pa
Śākyamuni

我佛釋迦牟尼尊號個個皆知知者無窮無盡惜乎悟者云稀

佛體金剛不壞趺
坐寶蓮世界慧心
靜觀自在能使羣
生愛戴

83 rDo rje'i snying pos rab tu 'joms pa
Vajragarbhapramardin

84 Rin chen 'od 'phro
Ratnārcis

佛光堪稱至寶破
除無限煩惱尊容
妙像莊嚴萬劫永
垂梨棗

85 Klu dbang gi rgyal po
Nāgeśvararāja

我佛稱號龍尊盤
滕默默無言慈光
四射絪縕阿誰叅
透因原

86 dPa' bo'i sde
Vīrasena

慧光普照乾坤精
進軍佛稱尊叅者
莫稍懈怠須當拔
樹尋根

87 dPal dgyes
Vīranandin

精進方能心喜佛
號大有所指衆生
被得洪恩實是淪
肌浹髓

88 Rin chen me
Ratnāgni

三昧是真是幻迷
者難詳難辨若要
窮究根由叩求寶
火佛案

89 Rin chen zla 'od
Ratnacandraprabha

一輪寶月光光佛
傳此號無疆蓮臺
端坐堂堂贍依大
是吉祥

90 mThong ba don yod
Amoghadarśin

善男子猛丈夫悟
禪機趣味殊不在
智不在愚此佛號
拔泥塗

91 Rin chen zla ba
Ratnacandra

一輪寶月在天我
佛把来作號放出
二指機關誰悟此
指消耗

端居清浄道塲煉
得慧根靈秀佛光
水月圓澄毫無微
塵之垢

92 Dri ma med pa
Vimala

93 dPal byin
Śūradatta

金身妙像威儀萬代頂禮無疑猛省勤修精進纔明吾佛勇施

性定清如止水心
空淨却微塵現出
本来面目一朶蓮
花化身

94 Tshangs pa
Brahmā

我佛清淨為施慈
悲推己及物衆生
苦志堅脩方得依
稀髣髴

95 Tshangs pas byin
Brahmadatta

天連水水接天佛
在中湛湛然叅得
透默會焉叅不透
歪厮纏

96 Chu lha
Varuṇa

97 Chu lha'i lha
Varuṇadeva

號稱水天中天吾
佛智慧無邊安居
九品金蓮何人悟
得真詮

98 dPal bzang
Bhadraśrī

尊號稱為賢德端
坐蓮臺默默如如
不動金身大展無
聲無色

栴檀香遍九天功
德撑持十地安然
高坐蓮臺妙喜吉
祥如意

99 Tsan dan dpal
Candanaśrī

100 gZi brjid mtha' yas
Anantaujas

雙耳垂肩妙像無
量掬光稱佛光風
霽月襟懷絶非凡
胎俗骨

101 ’Od dpal
Prabhāsaśrī

寶光根從大德大
德結就寶光兩手
傳来佛印善哉普
濟十方

102 Mya ngan med pa'i dpal
Aśokaśrī

與世開方便門引人入修行路自然生歡喜心永脫離煩惱趣

103 Sred med kyi bu
Nārāyaṇa

實訣不離兩手慧
澤沾遍人天叩問
吾佛聖號共稱曰
那羅延

104 Me tog dpal
Kusumaśrī

身似菩提寶樹自然功德生華結就因緣法果妙香遍滿金沙

105 Tshangs pa'i 'od zer rnam par rol bas mngon par mkhyen pa
Brahmajyotirvikrīḍitābhijña

我佛遊戲神通沐
浴清浄光中人人
信心頂禮永享極
樂無窮

106 Padma'i 'od zer rnam par rol bas mngon par mkhyen pa
Padmajyotirvikrīḍitābhijña

蓮花無異慧燈巍然安居上位若言吾佛神通不過遊戲三昧

107 Nor dpal
Dhanaśrī

法施財施具足大
千世界霑沐端為
衆生作福慈悲至
優至渥

108 Dran pa'i dpal
Smṛtiśrī

慈德常存念念一
體無全萬善度世
婆心一片爐爇名
香恭獻

109 mTshan dpal shin tu yongs sbgrags
Suparikīrtitanāmaśrī

萬善總歸一指鷲
嶺無窮妙喜善名
稱讚功德恒河沙
數難比

110 dBang po'i tog gi rgyal mtshan gyi rgyal po
Indraketudhvajarāja

紅熖放大毫光共
瞻禮帝幢王布宏
慈及萬方遍人天
沛澤長

111 Shin tu rnam par gnon pa'i dpal
Suvikrāntaśrī

雖稱善遊步佛却
是如如不動操持
慧劍跏趺功德阿
誰能懂

112 g'Yul las shin tu rnam par rgyal ba
Yuddhajaya

鬬戰勝却魔軍我
佛千年洪願修者
要悟慈心莫教六
賊滋蔓

113 rNam par gnon pa'i gshegs pa'i dpal
Vikrāntagāmiśrī

雖坐蓮臺不動寶
號稱善遊步周巡
寰宇無休一切衆
生普度

不肯滿着袈裟不
肯雙垂法履我佛
周匝莊嚴功德人
天歡喜

114 Kun nas snang ba bkod pa'i dpal
Samantāvabhāsavyūhaśrī

115 Rin chen padmas rnam par gnon pa
Ratnapadmavikrāmin

雖然遊步稱名其實何曾遊步寶華香遍三千行脚不離净土

116 Sangs rgyas ri dbang gi rgyal po
Śailendrarāja

我佛坐寶蓮花又
須彌山善住癡獃
分作兩岐難入宗
門覺路

心佛原無差別隨
應自然而然滿月
金容照現端居九
品香蓮

117 Sangs rgyas rje su spyod pa
Anucārin?-Buddha

118 Sangs rgyas mngon ’phags rgyal po
Abhyudgatarāja-Buddha

妙道顯而愈顯我
佛聖不自聖修成
顯聖法王常住西
方勝境

智光圓如實鏡慈輝四射無邊善滅諍譏之佛破盡野狐之禅

119 ’Khon dang (?) rgyags pa rnam gnon

120 Sangs rgyas rin chen gzugs bkod 'od snang
Ratnāṅgavyūhadyuti-Buddha

一體包羅萬寶淨
土莊嚴恁好時時
普放光輝照破衆
生煩惱

121 Sangs rgyas bdud dang yid gnyis kun 'joms (?)

魔障易生難滅我
佛威猛善滅鋪張
化日光天證得無
生無滅

122 Phyir mi ldog pa'i 'khor lo 'byung ba'i dpal
Avaivartikacakrasambhavaśrī?

當胸法寶持定不
廻吉祥輪名執着
不廻二字可是如
瞽如盲

123 Sangs rgyas rin gdugs 'phags
Ratnacchattrodgata-Buddha

八吉祥中一寶張
處撐持四大慈悲
覆冒衆生超度功
德為最

124 Sangs rgyas byang sems 'dul ba

慧劍滅却魔堆金
繩覺路宏開随引
菩提慈悲有緣得
脫凡胎

恐怖遠離顛倒夢
想究竟涅槃無畏
滅冥看破全無半
點遮闌

125 sKrag med mun bral rgyai po
Nirbhayavigatatamorāja?

126 Dang po sems skyed the tshom gcod mdzad
Prathamacittotpādasaṃśaya-cchedika?

世人礙于多疑所以不能入道我佛初慈决疑剖决上乘微妙

127 Sangs rgyas rnam gzigs
Vipaśyin

雙手一垂一仰大
道明如指掌家中
至寶常存啼鳥山
花供養

128 gTsug tor can
Śikhin

看来四大皆空一
身了無罣礙識破
撒手懸崖方悟金
身不壊

129 Thams cad skyob
Viśvabhū

大地一似浮漚要
悟不定而定可是
六勇尊佛攜手超
凡入聖

趺坐蓮臺自在如
如靜裡真宗瞻禮
拘留孫佛慧根超
脫愚蒙

130 'Khor ba 'jig
Krakucchanda

手印透出心印佛
心心佛如如萬殊
從来一本迷者較
量錙銖

131 gSer thub
Kanakamuni

一手搯来佛印真詮默地宣揚迦葉佛身証果端居極樂之鄉

132 ’Od bsrung
Kāśyapa

133 mTshan legs yongs grags dpal gyi rgyal po
Suparikīrtitanāmaśrīrāja

善名稱吉祥王大
慈悲登三寶結衆
生歡喜緣住西方
莊嚴好

134 Sangs rgyas rin po che dang zla ba dang padmas rab tu brgyan pa mkhas pa gzi brjid sgra dbyangs kyi rgyal po

Ratnacandrapadmapratimaṇḍita-paṇḍita?-tejaḥ-svaraghoṣarāja

智嚴寶月生光可
是大自在王如来
妙旨周詳誰能叅
透行藏

135 gSer bzang dri med rin chen snang brtul zhugs pa
Suvarṇabhadravimalaratnaprabhāsavrata

妙體煉成金色智
珠發出寶光妙行
端的成就極樂世
界無疆

無憂勝却煩惱如
来普現吉祥現身
在極樂地引人登
歡喜場

136 Mya ngan med mchog dpal
Aśokottamaśrī

137 Chos sgrags rgya mtsho'i dbyang
Dharmakīrtisāgaraghoṣa

性海澄如法海審
音永住雷音只此
本来面目何須根
外搜尋

138 Chos rgya mtsho mchog gi blos rnam par rol bar mngon par mkhyen pa'i rgyal po
Dharmasāgarāgra?matavikrīḍitābhijñārāja

遊戲何曽遊戲神
通大是神通法海
無邊勝慧要知非
色非空

139 sMan gyi bla bai dū rya'i 'od kyi rgyal po

Bhaiṣajyaguru-Vaiḍūryaprabhā-rāja

托鉢盂持貝葉琉璃光無生滅藥師王萬千刼稱如来西方歇

140 rGyal ba seng ge'i nga ro
Siṃhanāda

執得金鉢在手大地一聲獅吼不知獅吼之聲諸人能聽得否

法體妙證金剛寶
地安然不動執着
不動金剛可是未
醒癡夢

141 rDo rje mi ’khrugs pa
Vajrākṣobhya

142 ’Od zer kun ’phags dpal brtsegs rgyal po
Raśmisamudgataśrīkūṭarāja

偏袒稳坐昂藏積
成智慧金光光中
普現吉祥西方無
上法王

143 rGyal ba kun gzigs
Samantadarśin

拈来普慧之花香
色普充無際金身
普世皈依衆生普
沾慈惠

白毫放從寶頂靈
光普照羣迷掌裡
示人妙諦我佛微
露禪機

144 Rin chen gtsug tor can
Ratnaśikhin

145 'Jam dbyangs dkar po
Sita-Mañjughoṣa

两手開放蓮花花
裏金經慧劍善哉
大白文殊一泒慈
心普現

146 ’Jam dbyangs dpal gzhon nur gyur ba
Kumārabhūta-Mañjuśrī

特莊嚴童子身還
不離文殊號持慧
及斷羣邪無字經
傳妙道

147 ’Jam dbyangs brtan pa’i ’khor lo
Sthiracakra-Mañjughoṣa

文殊師利金身自能永住法輪右舉降魔寶劍左持無字靈文

148 ’Jam dbyang gsang sgrub
Guhyasādhana-Mañjughoṣa

魔盡方能成佛非
佛不能降魔借此
秘密機關看渠執
貝鳴螺

149 ’Jam dbyang seng ge’i sgra
Siṃhanāda-Mañjughoṣa

端拱跏趺蓮座當
胸一朵金蓮座下
獅王大吼一聲震
破人天

150 'Jam dbyang ngag gi rgyal po
Vādirāḍ-Mañjughoṣa

金身環遶蓮華常
住西方佛地文殊
幻相無窮寶號妙
語尊帝

151 'Jam dbyangs chos dbyings gsung gi dbang phyug brgyad pa
Aṣṭabhuja-Dharmadhātuvāgīśvara-Mañjughoṣa

十目十方共觀八
臂八方無礙法性
妙語圓通淨土文
殊自在

雙疊手跏趺坐定
了睛作功課此妙
音誰得聞此自在
誰參破

152 ’Jam dbyangs sgra bzang dbang phyug rgyal po
Bhadrasvareśvararāja-Mañjughoṣa

153 ’Jams dpal rgyal po rol ba
Rājalīlā-Mañjuśrī

遊戲却非遊戲自
在不著自在箇中
是耶非耶滋味阿
誰能解

154 'Jig gsum lhag par dbang du byed pa'i 'jam dbyangs
Trailokyavaśyādhikāra-Mañju-ghoṣa

三頭六臂巍然大
勝人天三界莊嚴
端坐蓮臺衆生虔
誠叩拜

155 mTshan brjod kyi 'jam dbyangs phyag bzhi pa
Caturbhuja-Nāmasaṃgīti-Mañjughoṣa

面面觀察六合手
手接引鴻恩端坐
靈山極樂千秋真
實名尊

156 'Jam dbyangs shes rab 'khor lo dang po
Prajñācakra-Mañjughoṣa

金經超脫羣迷慧
刄消除魔怪文殊
永轉慧輪萬刼金
身不壞

157 'Jam dpal rnon po
Ṭīkṣṇa-Mañjuśrī

四臂各持寶物巍
然敏捷文殊大展
慈悲度世衆生得
拔泥塗

合掌念念慈悲金
身毫光普放何須
甘露楊枝纔是觀
音本相

158 sPyan ras gzigs phyag bzhi pa
Caturbhuja-Avalokiteśvara

159 sPyan ras gzigs padma dbang 'byed
Padmavikāsana-Avalokiteśvara

不須楊柳枝頭開
遍妙蓮花朵大千
甘露均霑大士莊
嚴妙可

160 sPyan ras gzigs kha sar pa ni
Khasarpaṇa-Avalokiteśvara

如水清如月明觀
世音衆所稱度羣
迷救衆生紫竹林
化相呈

161 sPyan ras gzigs seng ge'i sgra
Siṃhanāda-Avalokiteśvara

調馴座下獅王大
是莊嚴威力普門
幻相誰叅想是善
財能識

162 ’Jig rten dbang phyug halhala
Hālāhala-Lokeśvara

幻像三頭六手騎
犼周行九有深意
阿誰分剖許汝脫
離塵垢

163 sPyan ras gzigs rdo rje chos
Vajradharma-Avalokiteśvara

六其手三其面惡
魔消慈心現金剛
身神而變微妙法
誰能辨

164 sPyan ras gzigs padma gar dbang phyag gnyis pa
Dvibhuja-Padmanarteśvara-Avalokiteśvara

降伏鏡裡魔軍大
作夢中佛事蓮花
妙舞稱揚自在觀
音大士

165 Padma gar dbang phyag bco brgyad pa
Aṣṭadaśabhuja-Padmanarteśvara

羅剎即是菩薩菩
薩刦非羅剎寶臂
一十有八蓮花妙
舞超拔

166 'Jig rten dbang phyug ha ri ha ri la zhon pa
Harihariv̄ahana-Lokesvara

不是文殊師利不
是三眼天魔騎犼
靜觀自在慈悲顯
相普陀

167 Khams gsum dbang ’dus spyan ras gzigs
Trailokyavaśaṃkara-Avalokiteśvara

權衡全賴大慈三
界視如平等無輕
無重如如法力天
人共領

168 ’Jig rten dbang phyug dmar po phyag bzhi pa
Caturbhuja-rakta-Lokeśvara

白衣化作紅光蓮
座如如自在暫拋
鸚鵡楊枝超出人
天三界

169 ’Jig rten dbang phyug mgrin sngon can
Nīlakaṇṭha-Lokeśvara

自在號尊青項萬
相不出一相聞聲
感應三千衆生頂
禮囬向

170 sGyu 'phrul dra ba'i rim pa'i spyan ras gzigs
Māyājālakrama-Avalokiteśvara

慈悲心夜义面變
金身重疊見甚深
法廣而幻普陀崖
稱妙善

171 Don yod zhags pa
Amoghapāśa

落伽化相無窮大
士名稱成鎖威嚴
警世慈悲超度無
分爾我

172 sPyan ras gzigs bhu kham dmar po
Mahābhūmika?-rakta-Avalokiteśvara

慧光照徹三界大
地遍覆紅雲伸手
慈懷接引普濟一
切迷津

八隻臂十一面大悲心神而幻紫竹林萬千變拔沉淪登彼岸

173 bCu gcig zhal
Ekādaśamukha[-Avalokiteśvara]

174 Nam mkha' rgyal po
Gaganarāja

十一首不為多十手也不為少要知幻相菩薩悟得虛空了了

175 sPyan ras gzigs sems nyid ngal gso
Cittaviśrāmaṇa-Avalokiteśvara

如意自在威儀端
然趺坐披衣金蓮
高聳瓔枝不須龍
女軍持

轉法輪持法貝大寶相莊嚴異離南海来濟世遇善緣皆如意

176 sPyan ras gzigs yid bzhin nor bu
Cintāmaṇi-Avalokiteśvara

177 sPyan ras gzigs rdo rje snying pos rab tu 'joms pa

Vajragarbhapramardin-Avalokiteśvara

落伽化現威儀超
出紅塵世界甚深
妙法無邊萬劫金
剛不壞

178 rDo rje khu tshur
Vajramuṣṭi

菩薩大慈大悲滿
握金剛拳印足令
龍象皈依頂禮金
容心信

179 rDo rje gnod sbyin
Vajrayakṣa

實號雖稱夜义却是慈容歡喜手中法器雙持誰識其中妙旨

180 rDo rje bsrung
Vajrarakṣa

慧光有感斯通妙
訣無微不度十方
一切含靈永賴金
剛保護

181 rDo rje las
Vajrakarma

寶杵能降外道金
鈴震醒群迷智行
普周十地衆生莫
不皈依

182 rDo rje smra ba
Vajrabhāṣa

金剛說法蓮臺百
萬人天瞻仰其如
示諸斯乎趺坐仰
伸雙掌

183 rDo rje rgyu
Vajrahetu

慈悲度盡人天結
成歡喜因緣手中
法寶誰傳如来妙
諦真詮

左持一卷金經右仗一枝慧劍金剛敏捷菩薩外道邪魔難見

184 rDo rje rnon po
Vajratīkṣṇa

185 rDo rje chos
Vajradharma

寶蓮擁護金身堪
稱金剛妙法仰賴
菩薩慈悲萬類同
登寶筏

186 rDo rje bzhad pa
Vajrahāsa

金容喜笑顏開破
除煩惱沉埋慈悲
度脫凡胎衆生共
躋春臺

187 rDo rje rgyal mtshan
Vajraketu

不是白傘蓋佛又
非增長天王借此
金剛幢蓋慈陰籠
罩十方

188 rDo rje gzi brjid
Vajratejas

手捧一輪寶鏡光
明遍照無邊菩薩
金剛德威恩輝具
足明圓

189 rDo rje rin chen
Vajraratna

欣然梵貝高擎自
是金剛大寶莊嚴
蓮座威儀永住西
天不老

190 rDo rje legs pa
Vajrasādhu

寶杵永鎮西天金
鈴妙偈真傳大悲
普度三千共頌金
剛善賢

191 rDo rje chags pa
Vajrarāga

坐引矢張弓穿
破迷闇普度菩薩
好箇威儀頂禮金
剛喜慕

192 rDo rje rgyal po
Vajrarāja

菩薩智慧無窮尊
號金剛大帝執此
如来法寶破盡邪
魔外祟

193 Byang chub rdo rje sems dpa'
Vajrasattva Bodhisattva

端拱持鈴在座金
剛勇識功課若問
妙諦真詮不離行
住坐卧

194 Byams pa phyag bzhi pa
Caturbhuja-Maitreya

三面三光對照四
臂四相領要不識
彌勒化身但看袒
腹微笑

195 Byams pa phyag gnyis pa
Dvibhuja-Maitreya

同瞻彌勒金身歡
喜世界生春左獻
如来法貝右展釋
帝金輪

196 Nam mkha' snying po
Ākāśagarbha

持寶珠比月圓光
遍滿虛空藏蓮座
上自跏趺度盡了
衆生障

197 Sa'i snying po
Kṣitigarbha

主張輪迴無竟地
藏法王妙用鏡花
點化手中指引泉
臺果証

198 Kun tu bzang po
Samantabhadra

端坐不言而笑普
賢菩薩神妙世界
雖是三千一點靈
光普照

色是空空是色除
諸障大功德寶鏡
輝開茅塞萬千秋
住佛國

199 sGrib pa rnam sel
Sarvanivaraṇaviṣkambhin

200 Kun tu bzang po glang chen po
Hastivāhana-Samantabhadra

座下白象調馴寶相莊嚴成就普賢大士神慈一切衆生蒙佑

201 sTong chen mo
Mahāsāhasrapramardanī

手持諸般法寶欲
度衆生了了佛母
摧碎大千超登多
羅三藐

坐蓮臺居極樂共
瞻仰大孔雀醒愚
蒙恩普博禮佛母
羣踴躍

202 rMa bya chen mo
Mahāmāyūrī

203 bSil ba'i tshal
Śītavatī

大寒林中佛母救衆生之疾苦功德周而遍普恒河沙兮難數

密咒隨持佛母救
濟無所不周執定
如来法海一任極
樂遨遊

204 gSang sngags rjes 'dzin
Mantrānusāriṇī

205 So sor 'brangs ma
Pratisarā

慈悲無處不周感
應隨人所求普遍
四大部洲金容萬
載長留

除盡諸般惡難殷
殷救度羣生寶座
金蓮高聳皈依極
樂同登

206 Seng ldeng nag 'bye sgrol ma
Khadiravaṇī-Tārā

207 Myur shing dpa’i sgrol ma
Pravīra?-Tārā

莊嚴尊者威儀速
勇稱為寶號仗茲
救度洪深破盡邪
魔外道

208 sGrol ma zla mdang ma
Candrakānti?-Tārā

瞻法相何精潔妙
莊嚴難盡說大善
心如秋月救度功
無休歇

209 sGrol ma gser mdog ma
Kanakavarṇa-Tārā

現十手之法相具
大慧之威儀仰金
色之實體施救度
之慈悲

210 gTsug tor sgrol ma
Uṣṇīṣa-Tārā

大地一切含靈遵
勝慈容共領寶礶
垂恩救度願把醍
醐灌頂

211 sGrol ma hūṃ sgra sgrogs ma
Hūṃsvaranādinī-Tārā

吽音遍布虛空可
是無邊無際大慈
救度三千百萬人
天益利

212 rNam par rgyal ba'i sgrol ma
Vijaya-Tārā

無遮無障無碍能
勝人天三界救度
佛母慈悲萬劫金
身長在

213 sGrol ma gzhan gyis mi thub pa
Aparājita-Tārā

慈力能摧惡敵金
繩慧及加持更把
法輪常轉普增佛
日光輝

214 sGrol ma bdud 'joms ma
Mārasūdana-Tārā

大智能摧怨魔萬
載衆生回向佛母
救度生靈大地沾
恩無量

救度百千萬刧寶
號湼槃寂滅除魔
降怪金身瑞靄祥
光朗徹

215 Mya ngan sel ba'i sgrol ma
Śokavinodana-Tārā

神索靈幡持握能
使諸邪攝伏世間
普賴佛緣慶誦靈
文備福

216 ’Gro ba ’gugs pa’i sgrol ma
Jagadvaśī?-Tārā

217 bKra shis skye ba'i sgrol ma
Maṅgalotpādana-Tārā

履正錫以迪吉作
善降之百祥以此
化脫衆生佛母惠
澤汪洋

218 sGrol ma smin byed ma
Pācaka-Tārā

火自心生如熾佛
母救度拯濟仰瞻
輪箭雙持滅刧邪
魔救世

219 sGrol ma khros ma nag mo
Kruddhakālī-Tārā

塵世誰来棒喝顰
眉威相我佛三頭
六臂金身立地惡
邪失魄

佛母號大柔善加
持慈悲念念救度
世上衆生一切俱
登彼岸

220 Zhi ba chen mo'i sgrol ma
Mahāśānti-Tārā

明咒吽聲救度佛母恩光無礙那有外道邪魔萬載衆生頂戴

221 Chags pa 'joms pa'i sgrol ma
Rāganisūdana-Tārā

蓮座香騰貝葉手捧鏡光不輟度脱衰敗衆生照徹不生不滅

222 bDe ba sbyin pa'i sgrol mo
Sukhada-Tārā

一手高擎何物三
手垂伸何故能動
三界金身慈悲救
度佛母

223 sGrol ma rnam par rgyal ma dkar mo
Sita-Vijaya-Tārā

佛法無量無邊覆
被毫無分別佛燈
照徹三千諸苦立
地消滅

224 sDug bsngal bsregs pa'i sgrol ma
Duḥkhadahana-Tārā

225 dNgos grub stsol ba'i sgrol ma
Siddhida-Tārā

佛法無巨無細不二門中真諦手捧一盞慧燈光射大千無際

吉祥圓滿救度極
樂西方長住佛母
寶礶端持盛貯醍
醐甘露

226 Yongs su rdzogs pa'i sgrol ma
Paripūrṇa-Tārā?

佛母除諸惡毒感
應人天迅速衆生
盡在覆育瞻禮金
身丈六

227 Dug nag sel ba'i sgrol ma
Jāṅgulī-Tārā

228 Gur las gzungs pa'i rdo rje sgrol ma
[Vajra]pañjarabhāṣita-Vajratārā

救度佛母多名此位金剛宮室天花散布人天法力神通祕密

229 rGya nag rim pa'i sgrol ma
Cīnakrama-Tārā

足下攝伏魔祟舉
劍神威可畏震旦
救度生靈誰曉箇
中滋味

三目通徹三光如
意寶輪度世蓮臺
笑拈曇花法像天
開雲霽

230 sGrol dkar yid bzhin gyi 'khor lo
Cintāmaṇicakra-sita-Tārā

佛母如意自在救度蒼生依賴如如不染纖塵全仗慈悲覆蓋

231 Yid bzhin rgyal mo phyag bzhi ma
Caturbhuja-Cintāmaṇirājñī

232 sGrol dkar phyag drug ma
Ṣaḍbhuja-sita-Tārā

叅禮西方佛母不
是化相觀音幻就
三頭六臂白衣萬
載稱尊

233 sGrol ma nor sbyin ma
Dhanada-Tārā

摩尼珠掌中陳捧
一冊無字文布金
田救度殷援群生
出迷津

除盡諸般惡趣救
度佛母恳該净掃
泥犁疾苦共教合
掌蓮臺

234 Ngan song las sgrol ba'i sgrol ma
Durgottāriṇī-Tārā

235 Don thams cad sgrub pa'i sgrol ma
Sarvārthasādhana-Tārā

一切善緣成就幻
相神威靈佑足下
收伏邪魔大地衆
生普救

神其威定其性大
而化明而聖諸惡
毒除清淨顯威靈
在佛境

236 ’Phags ma dug sel ma
Ārya-Jāṅgulī

237 lHa mo ral gcig phyag nyi shu rtsa bzhi ma
Caturviṃśatibhuja-Ekajaṭā

億劫尊稱佛母二
十四臂金身一髻
皈依萬法要知我
佛能仁

無相方成諸相跏
趺九品金蓮要把
釋迦寶諦掌中秘
示真傳

238 sNa chogs yum
Viśvamātṛ

二臂一髻慈和衆
生受益良多慧光
千載難磨焚香虔
誦南無

239 lHa mo ral gcig ma
Ekajaṭā

雙手示顯佛花雙手金鉢捧定瞻依四臂準提永住西方聖境

240 lHa mo tsundā p̱hyag bzhi ma
Caturbhuja-Cundā

手手不離法寶端
居足踏蓮葩廣臂
準提佛母慈容萬
刼堪誇

241 lHa mo tsundā phyag mang
Bahubhuja-Cundā

242 'Od zer can phyag bcu ma
Daśabhuja-Mārīcī

兩手護持日月積
得佛光照徹金身
高駕仙車萬姓志
心叩謁

三界照臨三面八臂護持八方秘受如來多寶佛母號稱積光

243 ’Od zer can phyag brgyad ma
Aṣṭabhuja-Mārīcī

積成三昧佛光照
徹幽明因果座下
白象調馴掌握妙
蓮一朵

244 ’Od zer can phyag gnyis ma
Dvibhuja-Mārīcī

245 'Od zer can bdud rtsi'i ma
Mārīcī

足踏邪魔伏首變
象威靈知否多般
法寶堅持制服毒
龍在手

246 ’Od zer can rdo rje dbyings kyi dbang phyug ma
Vajradhātvīśvarī-Mārīcī

極樂世界佛母煉
就金剛智性頂禮
寶像莊嚴積得慧
光上乘

247 gTsug tor rnam rgyal ma
Uṣṇīṣavijayā

寶礶滿貯醍醐掌
托佛身清淨三千
大千之中無人不
理尊勝

248 ’Phags ma gdugs dkar po can
Ārya-Sitātapatrā

化相威超三界尊
號曰白傘盖度群
生咸依賴大功德
同覆載

249 Lo ma gyon ma phyag drug ma
Ṣaḍbhuja-Parṇaśabarī

皈依葉衣佛母裝
嚴何必袈裟制伏
邪魔外道三頭六
臂光華

金容看去猙獰一片慈心聖善葉衣佛母尊嚴一切含靈稱贊

250 Lo ma gyon ma phyag bzhi ma
Caturbhuja-Parṇaśabarī

251 Sher phyin phyag gnyis ma
Dvibhuja-Prajñāpāramitā

尊般若號佛母救
生靈諸疾苦妙蓮
花生浄土捧金經
誓願普

身似菩提寶樹心
存般若波羅大展
我佛寶卷慧光度
世云多

252 Sher phyin phyag bzhi ma
Caturbhuja-Prajñāpāramitā

253 rDo rje dbyangs can ma phyag drug ma
Ṣaḍbhuja-Vajrasarasvatī

特在極樂西方幻
化三頭六臂但知
金剛妙音誰解佛
母妙諦

254 rDo rje dbyangs can ma phyag gnyis ma
Dvibhuja-Vajrasarasvatī

手執金經一卷不
知有字無字瞻仰
金剛妙音好與吾
佛無異

佛母端坐蓮花懷
中震動琵琶妙音
普遍恒沙慈悲感
應無涯

255 Pi wang dbyangs can ma
Vīṇā-Sarasvatī

256 lHa mo khro gnyer can ma
Bhṛkuṭī

寶塔玲瓏在手顰
眉作號知否慈悲
救度婆心頂禮天
高地厚

257 rDo rje tsa rtsig
Vajracarcikā

座下收伏魔頭可
是佛母威力寶號
匝呼訾嘎普度無
窮無極

258 Sor 'brangs phyag gnyis ma
Dvibhuja-Pratisarā

慧劍斬斷魔頭金
輪光照九州慈悲
隨人所求救度無
所不周

259 Phyir bzlog ma
Mahāpratyaṅgirā

慧劍持法輪轉舉
金鉤執寶傘妙蓮
花手中展佛母容
寶冠冕

260 rGyal mtshan rtse mo'i dpung rgyan
Dhvajāgrakeyūrā

法相威而不猛慈
心化而通神幢頂
髆嚴佛母慈悲顯
化金身

261 gZhan gyis mi thub ma
Aparājitā

妙智神光無敵妝
伏邪魔清淨慧光
焰焰騰輝位列西
天上聖

262 rDo rje gandha ri
Vajragāndhārī

手中法器多般無
非降魔至寶萬衆
合掌皈依歡喜永
除煩惱

263 Chos kyi rdo rje ma
Dharmavajrī

修得無窮妙法淨
土不染纖塵佛母
金剛性智拯拔一
切沉淪

264 Las kyi rdo rje ma
Karmavajrī

上透三十三天下
遍十八地獄大悲
無處不周智行金
剛具足

265 Sems ma rdo rje ma
Sattvavajrī

勇是非常神勇識
則無邊大識西天
佛母靈通涵育群
生無極

266 Rin chen rdo rje ma
Ratnavajrī

好箇大寶金剛一
位巍巍法王頂上
放白毫光慧明照
耀十方

267 lHa mo shra ma ṇa
Śramaṇā

不在蓮臺端坐立
地接引衆生沙羅
門為實號萬姓頂
戴虔誠

268 Nor sbyin ma
Dhanadā

佛母大慈大悲萬
類均沾化育閻浮
世界衆生普遍受
茲長祿

269 gZa' yum
Grahamātṛkā

法相位尊北極靈
明感應無差端坐
布金世界塵寰普
染光華

270 Pad dkar shes rab gsal byed
Prajñālokakṛtya-sita-Vajravārāhī

法貝滿盛甘露寶
旛接引人天明慧
金剛亥母白毫光
射無邊

271 Phag mo don thams cad sgrub pa
Sarvārthasādhana-Vārāhī

足踏妖魔鎮定亥
母金剛智行成就
一切功德妙道堪
稱堪慶

272 Yan lag 'byung
Aṅgaja

拂子掃盡塵霾爐
烟薫陶世界慈悲
徧被人天度脫了
無障碍

273 Ma pham pa
Ajita

削髮因除煩惱留
鬚為表文夫普度
世間無量渾如化
相文殊

274 Nags na gnas
Vaṇavāsin

位證西方極樂拂
子手中拈着伐那
婆斯尊者普度皈
依正覺

275 Dus ldan
Kālika

两手分執雙環應
是調獅馴象位證
尊者大名無不皈
依法相

276 rDo rje mo'i bu
Vajrīputra

拂子指揮如意心
心念念菩提座列
軍持甘露誰叅尊
者機微

跋陀羅羣頂戴瞻
法相大自在度衆
生三千界信心殷
共展拜

277 bZang po
Bhadra

278 gSer bi'u
Kanakavatsa

迦諾迦伐蹉尊跏趺蓮臺不動雙球兩手分持好箇慈悲面孔

279 Ba ra dhwā dza gser can
Kanakabharadvāja

靄靄祥雲護體誰
悟尊者就裡如如
在在禅心皓月清
風可比

280 Ba ku la
Bakula

危坐一手問訊放
出毫光如鏡端的
尊者儀容令人瞻
依起敬

281 sGra gcan 'dzin
Rāhula

雙手端拱在座一切有無看破號稱羅沽羅尊應是西方首坐

282 Lam phran
Cūḍapanthaka

慈容歡喜生春婆
心永無休歇注茶
半托尊者萬載無
生無滅

283 Ba ra dhwā dza bsdod snyoms les
Piṇḍolabharadvāja

座畔金經数卷手
探鉢裡醍醐想為
衆生濟拔洗滌一
切煩枯

一册金經在手箇中多少禪機若問有字無字唯有尊者能知

284 Lam bstan
Panthaka

285 Klu'i sde
Nāgasena

坐攜九環錫杖爐
中香靄絪緼制伏
毒龍在座同瞻那
迦犀尊

286 sBed byed pa
Gopaka

手捧一卷金經莫
認語言文字戒博
迦尊者容大露禪
機妙意

手托着靈山塔靈山塔在心頭阿秘特婆心切諸煩惱一時休

287 Mi phyed pa
Abheda

288 dGe bsnyen dha rma ta la
Upāsaka-Dharmatāla

負經函執拂子現
佛身生歡喜伏猛
虎隨衣履大功行
應無比

289 Hwa shang dge bsnyen
Upāsaka-Hwa-shang

寶號蓮花妙舞面
龎幻化神奇成就
金剛法體千秋萬
載名垂

290 ’Od bsrung chen po
Mahākāśyapa

曾與阿難尊者相
共對侍蓮臺化像
湛然端坐心心常
向如来

終朝侍從如來因
得如来妙諦特來
趺坐蓮臺指點迷
途開示

291 Kun dga' bo
Ānanda

性字三

292 Sha na'i gos can
Śāṇakavāsin

不是普門化相竹
林妙現慈悲指示
人天覺路共稱是
沙納衣

293 Nyer sbas
Upagupta

一箇金鉢在手五蘊四大皆空優婆俱多在座千秋大闡宗風

搭其手盤其足度世心優而渥妙蘭葩散芬馥得此味受清福

294 Dhi dhi ka
Dhītika

穩坐蒲團一箇披
衣灌想功課此味
有誰嚐過叩求慈
悲説破

295 Nag po
Kāla

296 Legs mthong
Sudarśana

善觀善觀自在端
坐蓮花世界伸掌
若有所思此意阿
誰能解

化成猙獰法像制
伏脚底一象護持
道法威名萬劫巍
巍蕩蕩

297 mGon po phyag drug pa
Ṣaḍbhuja-Mahākāla

298 ’Brong zhal can

佛法全憑護法牛首猛若金剛極樂塲中安享沙門勇保無疆

299 Ṭa kṣad seng ge zhon pa
Siṃhavāhana-Ṭakṣad

渾如師利化身調
攝獅王安靜多般
法貝隨身護法西
方勝境

300 mGon po ṭa kṣad-?
Mahākāla-Ṭakṣad

騎天馬執法寶覩
金容莊嚴好震雄
威稱勇保護妙法
常不老

301 mGon po stag zhon
Vyāghravāhana-Mahākāla

手中舉定金錘調
馴山王頂刻仗此
勇保護法永鎮佛
門赫赫

302 mGon po legs ldan
Bhagavad-Mahākāla

善德勇保護法劍
鉢不離兩手伏魔
足下神威永住西
天悠久

303 mGon po beng
Daṇḍa[dhara]-Mahākāla

持棒永住佛門勇
保西方極樂護法
神威耿耿毫無矯
揉造作

304 Las mgon bya rog gdong can
Kākāsya-Karmanātha

不是孔雀明王不是大鵬護法面稱慈烏威嚴念念慈悲救拔

305 mGon po gur
Mahākāla-pañjara?

脚踏魔王歸服手
中法寶二事宮室
勇保護法令人五
體投地

306 mGon po phyag bzhi pa
Caturbhuja-Mahākāla

一劍制服妖邪一
傘覆臨萬類佛門
護法威靈妙旨誰
能叅會

307 Zhal bram gzugs
Brāhmaṇarūpa[-Mahākāla]

寶傘張施慈蔭梵
音震動喧喧佛法
全資護法頗羅門
號稱尊

大黑雄威護法端
然穩駕良驥手持
法貝金鎗一切怪
魔藏避

308 Ṭa kṣad nag po
Kṛṣṇa-Ṭakṣad

309 lHa mo dong skyong ma
Śaṅkhapālī

現慈容無爾我妙
莊嚴無不可頂螺
稱成妙果大慈悲
羣感荷

310 lHa mo dong sol ma
Dhūmāvatī

法體神而又神能
烘諸敵施仁天母
護法金身功行圓
滿精純

311 dPal ldan lha mo phyag gnyis ma
Dvibhuja-śrīmatī-Devī

頂上祥生寶盖慈
悲無所不周暫離
蓮臺趺坐欲從四
大巡遊

312 Chos rgyal
Dharmarāja

一時魔怪全降服
德畏威普濟正道
仰賴維持莫不皈
依法帝

尊號宜帝護法雄
威赫赫原殊保護
梵天正道許多外
道蠲除

313 Ṭa kki ra dza
Ṭakkirāja

314 Dzi na mi ṭra
Jinamitra

實器中藏甘露法
皷震動天人可是
恒河沙界瞻依莫
不尊親

妙相威嚴赫奕雄
風耀武婆娑護國
又兼護法佛門萬
載難磨

315 Kṣe tra pa la
Kṣetrapāla

316 Tshe bdag mgon po
Āyuṣpati-Mahākāla

六臂持来法器永
護佛門左右欽羡
廣大神通普度衆
生仁壽

像猙獰心善慈除
魔障惠澤垂衆法
寶任施爲閻浮世
盡稱奇

317 mGon dkar yid bzhin nor bu
Sita-Cintāmaṇi-Mahākāla

318 rNam sras tshe ’phel dkar po
Sita-Āyurvardhana-Vaiśravaṇa

護法将獅騎了度
脱衆生煩擾大白
祝壽財寶利益人
天多少

319 rNam sras drag byed nag po
Raudra-kṛṣṇa-Vaiśravaṇa

把慧劍挺金戈馳
天馬舞婆娑貫介
冑震邪魔佑生靈
利益多

320 rGyal chen rnam thos sras
Mahārāja-Vaiśravaṇa

靈通寶傘端持奕
禩佛門永鎮妙哉
財寶天王萬類同
沾庇蔭

堪作佛門上将人
人瞻仰大雄戟鉞
寶幢護法維持吾
佛宗風

321 rNam sras mdong dmar
Raktaśūla-Vaiśravaṇa

322 rNam sras ser chen
Mahāpīta-Vaiśravaṇa

座下獅王大吼寶
盖高擎在手護持
妙道悠久金色莊
嚴不朽

323 Sa'i lha mo brtan ma
Dṛḍhā-Pṛthivī

寳礶醍醐滿貯經
行四大部洲地主
永寧天母慈悲恩
德難酬

324 rNam sras gar mkhan mchog
Nartakavara-Vaiśravaṇa

披金甲馭飛龍稱
妙舞現慈容護正
法保真宗享極樂
功德隆

325 ’Phags skyes po
Virūḍhaka

寶劍能驅諸惡尊
號增長天王智慧
雄威兼具發願永
鎮西方

326 sPyan mi bzang
Virūpākṣa

手托靈山寶塔心
存多寶如來廣目
天王大願萬年長
護蓮臺

327 Yul 'khor bsrung
Dhṛtarāṣṭra

持國天王寶號琵
琶端執當胸震響
梵音普被法門永
護無窮

328 brGya byin
Śatakratu

心存接引人天好
個帝釋寶像法螺
兩手高擎喚醒癡
修妄想

329 Tshangs pa
Brahman

不指天不指地轉
法輪引羣類梵王
恩人天備使衆生
感寤寐

330 lHa mo tsaṇḍi ka
Caṇḍikā

本是面慈心善法
相聖而且神向朁
芝噶天母拈香展
拜頻頻

法體裝成羅刹陽
和澤溥宏仁一片
慈悲濟度歡喜天
母值春

331 dPyid kyi lha mo
Vasanta-devī

332 dByar gyi lha mo
Varṣā-devī

手中佛寶加持護
法威靈妙也心與
造化同功全資天
母值夏

護法騎来仙鹿手持靈寶遨遊法相幻而非幻瞻依天母值秋

333 sTon gyi lha mo
Śarad-devī

334 dGun gyi lha mo
Hemanta-devī

一手收来法海虔
誠頂禮慈容成就
佛門功行萬劫天
母值冬

吉祥長壽天母護
法佛門無疆賴此
慈悲因果衆生長
壽吉祥

335 bKra shis tshe ring ma
Maṅgaladīrghāyus

336 Beg tse

口近一朶青蓮大
紅勇保名高脚下
魔怪全收可是護
法功勞

337 Dur khrod bdag po
Citipati

不同面然大士金
身幻作髑髏慈悲
九幽度徹誰叅就
裡根由

338 Mi g'yo ba sngon po
Nīla-Acala

青青不動金剛慧
刄外道全降金身
普散毫光梵天長
享安康

339 Dzam bha la ser po
Pīta-Jambhala

觀黃布禄金剛莊
嚴委寶唐皇法施
財施具足人天利
益無疆

340 Mi g'yo ba dkar po
Sita-Acala

金剛號稱不動寶
劍威震西天位證
佛門大器善因妙
果兼全

341 Dzam bha la phyag drug pa
Ṣaḍbhuja-Jambhala

法體三頭六臂金
容濡露慈悲布祿
恩先廣被人人莫
不皈依

342 Khro bo stobs po che
Krodhamahābala

賴此大力金剛震
動神威無比頂禮
赫赫金容恩德淪
肌浹髓

343 'Jig rten gsum rgyal
Trailokyavijaya

至實無所不持佛
境優游自在功行
遍滿恒沙金剛能
勝三界

344 Dzam bha la nag po
Kṛṣṇa-Jambhala

足下邪魔收伏筭
来功行無邊黑布
禄金剛體衆生頂
禮誠虔

金繩覺路宏開滅
怪除魔清淨伏兹
寶杵靈通振作佛
門畢竟

345 Gegs mthar byed
Vighnāntaka

346 bDud rtsi 'khyil pa
Amṛtakuṇḍalin

金剛甘露為潭跏
趺大妙莊嚴天人
萬類均霑端然永
侍瞿曇

347 rDo rje lcags sgrog ma
Vajraśṛṅkhalā

六臂撐持六合三
目慧映三光具足
無邊法力方稱金
鐲金剛

傳来佛寶多般法
相萬年無損八猴
不動金剛生靈仰
賴接引

348 Mi g'yo ba spre'u brgyad pa
Aṣṭakapi-Acala

349 Me ltar ’bar ba
Jvālānala

狰獅丈六金身普
照慧光烈焰金剛
法力宏深好把怪
魔煅煉

350 Mi g'yo ba phyag bzhi pa
Caturbhuja-Acala

看去威猛形容原
來不動姿格千秋
功行宏深豈是一
朝一夕

351 Khro mo sme brtsegs

寶號共稱威積慈
容大是雍和寶礶
醍醐在手消除世
界煩痾

352 rDo rje rnam ’joms
Vajravidāraṇī

執金鈴杵在手歡
喜容慈恩厚摧碎
了衆生咎住西天
稱佛母

353 Zhang blon rdo rje bdud 'dul

醫藥大權伏魔萬
年護法西天衆生
五體投地慈悲疾
困都蠲

354 gNod sbyin gang ba bzang po
Yakṣa-Pūrṇabhadra

全裝甲冑威風護
法功德不淺騎來
天馬巡遊共誦夜
义賢滿

355 Dzam bha la dkar po 'brug zhon
Sita-nāgavāhana-Jambhala

座下飛龍獨跨遊
行四大部洲布向
世間天祿慈悲無
所不周

三頭六臂金剛無
限天威畢積許多
法寶加持救度羣
生大益

356 Khro bo sme brtsegs

357 Seng gdong ma
Siṃhavaktrā

幻就獅王面目大
慈大悲為心佛母
神威大力自然魔
怪難侵

358 bCom ldan reg tshig
Bhagavad-Bhayanāśana

金剛諸障能烘永
侍梵王之宮寶像
若箇能通包涵至
道無窮

359 rDo rje hūṃ mdzad
Vajrahūṃkāra

两手鈴杵交持四
面神光茪蔚金剛
一吽威聲多少妖
魔退畏

一十二臂昂藏梵
王異相金剛靈寶
授自西方共稱紅
部落王

360 Tshogs bdag dmar chen
Mahārakta-Gaṇapati

Index